MY LIFE VALUES I

- described in 21 Reflections and 97 Food for Thought

George Manus

Author: George Manus
Copyright: George Manus
Design and Layout: Ole Praud

Publisher: BoD • Books on Demand GmbH, In de Tarpen 42, 22848 Norderstedt, Tyskland
Printing: Libri Plureos GmbH, Friedensallee 273, 22763 Hamborg, Tyskland

George's online bookstore:
- www.georgemanus-books.com

The Art of George Manus online store:
- www.georgemanus.com

George's Innovation & hub website:
- www.maxmanusinnovation.com

George Manus e-mail:
info@georgemanus.com

ISBN: 978-87-4305-920-2

Other books written by George Manus

THOUGHTS	English
TANKER	Norwegian
REFLECTIONS I	English
REFLEKSJONER I	Norwegian
REFLECTIONS II	English
REFLEKSJONER II	Norwegian
REFLECTIONS III	English
REFLEKSJONER III	Norwegian
A WOMAN'S MANY MIGRATIONS	English
EN KVINNES MANGE FLYTTINGER	Norwegian
STORIES & THOUGHTS I	English
HISTORIER OG TANKER I	Norwegian
STORIES & THOUGHTS II	English
HISTORIER OG TANKER II	Norwegian
INNOVATIONS AND CREATIONS	English
MAX MANUS FIRMAENE -70 år i kommunikasjon	Norwegian
WORDS FOR THE ROAD - ORD MED PÅ VEIEN I	English - Norwegian
WORDS FOR THE ROAD - ORD MED PÅ VEIEN II	English - Norwegian
WORDS FOR THE ROAD - ORD MED PÅ VEIEN III	English - Norwegian
WORDS FOR THE ROAD - ORD MED PÅ VEIEN IV	English - Norwegian
WORDS FOR THE ROAD - ORD MED PÅ VEIEN V	English - Norwegian
WORDS FOR THE ROAD - ORD MED PÅ VEIEN VI	English - Norwegian
WORDS FOR THE ROAD - ORD MED PÅ VEIEN VII	English - Norwegian
WORDS FOR THE ROAD - ORD MED PÅ VEIEN VIII	English - Norwegian
WORDS FOR THE ROAD - ORD MED PÅ VEIEN IX	English - Norwegian
WORDS FOR THE ROAD - ORD MED PÅ VEIEN X	English - Norwegian
FOOD FOR THOUGHTS - 1001 Short reflections	English
TANKEVEKKERE - 1001 korte refleksjoner	Norwegian
217 REFLECTONS - Reflections on big and small	English
217 REFLEKSJONER - Refleksjoner over stort og smått	Norwegian
THE MISCHIEVOUS BOY - and The War Hero	English
RAMPEGUTTEN - og Krigshelten	Norwegian
MINE LIVSVERDIER I	Norwegian
MINE LIVSVERDIER II	Norwegian

Introduction

March 23

In this first book of two, which in no way purports to be a pedagogical textbook, I have selected 21 Reflections from my book "217 Reflections", published in 2020. All of them are in one way or another related to "Essential Life Values and Challenges". The first was written in 1990 and the last in 2023. They were put on paper to test my opinions and thoughts about Life Values and Challenges.

The 97 Food for Thought are collected from my book: "Food for Thought - 1001 short reflections", published in 2020. They are inserted after each Reflection and related to these.

Both books are intended to give you an insight to how I look at life values and challenges.

Many of my Reflections are very personal and were never meant to be publicized in this way. However, they have now been put together in these two books, because of feedback I have received from people who has read both my Reflections and Food for Thought books.

Honest self-awareness gives you a solid platform to stand on in life; it is a gift not given to all.

Many must work towards that goal themselves, like I have done, and this is where this book, as an example, shows you how I have exposed my honest self-awareness.

Read, digest, and take a rest.
Compare with your own thoughts and pick out the best.

Your self-awareness will thus be strengthened, and your platform more solid and firm,
making solving life's challenges easier in turn.

Only by reading slowly and with dedication will you benefit from using this book to help you face life's challenges.

In my opinion and based on my assumptions, I have long had the ideology in life that, just as surely as we are different and have our own personal identity, the Creator has given us the opportunity to choose between two diametrically different types of life, the Good and the Evil.

As I am not a fan of black/white solutions, it becomes more nuanced when I say that with extended self-awareness, we can decide for ourselves where on the scale between the two extremes we want to be. The choice is up to us.

Fanaticism is the starting point for wrong views, so in this context, the two extreme types of life, the Good or the Evil, will turn out to be conflict-creating.

By reading my personal Reflections and the short Food for Thought, you will quickly understand that I would like to appear firmly rooted in the Good lifestyle.

In my eighty-fifth year, I am still working on the fine-tuning. Nothing is perfect in life.

I would be very happy if you can find inspiration in this book, for expanded thoughts which can give you better self-confidence and a more solid platform to stand on when facing life's challenges.

I recommend keeping the book on hand and using it when you are at a crossroad in life.

DEDICATION

May these books become inspiration, guidance, and reflection for **my family descendants** on their own life's journey. "My Life Values I and II" are written with love, hope and based on my experience over a long period. Find strength and joy in living according to Life Values that are important to you and yours.

THE MIDDLE WAY

The answer is always the Middle Way.
So, it was with Aristotle and so it is today.
Not too much greed and not too much spending.
Not too aggressive and not too defending.
Not too evil and not too good.
This is what I have understood.

1995

MY LIFE VALUES I
- described in 21 Reflections and 97 Food for Thought

George Manus

The following is my recommendation on how to maximize the book's benefits, be it through group discussion, life coaching or as an individual reader

1. Read or discuss all the "Reflections" and note those that are most relevant to you, considering your own personal values at the same time.

2. Set aside the ones not relevant to you now, and concentrate on the ones that are relevant.

3 Take a good look on the associated "Food for Thought" and form an opinion about this.

4 Compare my view of the Reflection in question, with yours.

4 Form opinions on the Reflections you have read/discussed and take a note of them.

5 Follow this procedure for each Reflection that you feel is important to you.

From this solid platform you have now created for yourself, you will have become more aware and self-confident of how to face life's challenges.

IMPORTANT INFORMATION!

Note the date below the heading of the Reflection you are reading, where it is given.

From this you will understand that my Reflections span more than 30 years, meaning that the content has been created in step with challenges that I, like everyone else have faced.

AMBITIONS AND THE SUB-GOAL

April 2013

Not everyone possesses a competitive spirit. This, among other things, is what ambition stands for, "the desire to compete, aspiration".

It all has to do with yourself. As with prestige, it is something personal. But it does not necessarily have the same negative connotations as prestige in my opinion.

"The desire to compete, aspiration", I see here not necessarily as being in competition with others.

I choose, at least for the time being, to look at wanting to compete as something you want to do for yourself, compete with yourself and whatever ambitions you might have in each situation.

Here the driving force comes into it again. Where there's no driving force, it's difficult to find progress.

Of course, lots of people are happy without having ambitions. Why do so many people see being without ambition as something negative? Imagine what the world would be like if everyone had limitless ambitions?

I think we all agree that not everyone can be academically inclined. What about the countless number of service jobs needed to get the world to function? It shouldn't, in any way, mean that someone is worth less or lacks ambitions just because they aren't academically inclined.

Society ought to function in such a way, that those who have personal ambitions should basically be able to achieve them.

Sporting ambitions, if they only concern yourself, are both necessary and correct to have. If your ambition is to reach the top, then many self-denials and sacrifices are necessary; if you aren't motivated and don't have steel-clad ambitions, you simply won't reach your goal.

It is worse when parents have ambitions on behalf of their children.

I begin with some personal experiences from my early days in business.

Before I turned twenty at the end of the fifties, I was already responsible for the training of approximately 40 technicians.

Even then, I noticed that many of those who already had families fought hard to give their children an education, as they felt they themselves had not been able to have one due to the war.

It was a matter of course, that if it hadn't been for the war, they would all have done their A-levels, gone to university, and ended up with important positions.

Following the war, children without the necessary abilities were practically forced to get an education they weren't suited for, and often ended up with big problems. Many family tragedies unfolded because of the often well-meaning but misguided ambitions parents had on behalf of their children.

The worst examples of this – the sports ambitions of parents for their children – I personally witnessed later.

I was reminded of this the other day, during a conversation with our local golf pro.

The golf club had just finished a golfing event organized by the Spanish Golf Federation with participants of both genders, in the so- called "Juvenile" class, from 8 to 16.

He just shook his head in despair at how he had seen various examples of over ambitious parents dominating these children and youngsters during practice, resulting in both tears and the gnashing of teeth.

My own examples are similar when it comes to both tennis and skiing, and from the time when my daughters were growing up and were, of course, members of the local clubs for these sporting activities.

This was in Oslo in Norway and took place on the so-called better west-side where we lived.

You could at times witness literally horrific incidents. I even had to cancel my daughters' memberships at the local tennis club due to its over ambitious leadership. The example is too grotesque to mention, as it didn't directly involve my daughters.

It was not uncommon to see parents who, during simple slalom competitions, threw themselves out onto the slope when one of their hopefuls fell, with an outburst of excuses that they had wrongly waxed the skis, or that the fall had been caused by badly sharpened steel edges.

That you want to see your descendants be successful is obviously human, but with this type of ambition it backfires all too often.

I have included a reflection called: The sub-goal, related

to my own sporting ambitions in golf, which I wrote in August 1995. I call it the sub-goal because my intuition tells me that it'll become a sub-goal, even though it has been the main goal up until now.

The happy day, the 9th of August 1995. The goal which seemed impossible to achieve, has been reached.

Oh well, it probably never seemed impossible to achieve; but there's no doubt of it having been high up and a long way away before being reached.

I've just got home from the golf course, Bogstad. It's close to half past nine in the evening and the obligatory bath has been carried out.

Now I'm wandering quietly around the dining-room table with a towel around my waist, in an eternal circle, Pocket Memo in hand.

Totally relaxed and with a wonderful feeling in my body.

"Single figure handicap".

The goal has finally been reached. The number 9, not two numbers, just the one. How in the world can it be that something so insane as a tiny number, can be of such importance in this context? Only to yourself, of course.

Just two simple little strokes separate me from my previous handicap, which was 11 – just two strokes. Whether they're 200 metres or 30 centimetres is of no importance, the fact is that we're only talking about 2 strokes in 36 holes.

Ideally speaking 36 holes should normally be completed in 72 strokes, with a minimal variation depending on the difficulty of each course.

I have opened a bottle of red wine and lit the two candles on the table. I'm waiting for the chicken to heat up. The rice is almost ready and in one or two minutes I'll let the peace flow through me.

It was a fantastic round. Impossible for a non-golfer to comprehend, but when I think of having played the course in 77 strokes, five over par for the course, I can barely believe it's true.

It all happened in a Thursday match under perfect conditions, where I, with my 11-handicap, played to 42 Stableford points.

Now I understand once again what it means, what the meaning of the thesis I so often use is, namely that: "It's not the goal that's important, it's the process that counts".

Now I've reached my goal, but I realize that from this moment on, it has become a sub-goal. "Single figure handicap", I'll look upon from this day on as a sub-goal and not the goal itself, as just one of the many steps in the stairway. That's how it is. How many steps the stairway has is unimportant. Figuratively speaking, it could be an infinite number. The thought of what my next sub-goal in golf should be, is unclear.

Will I ever be able to repeat the result or, better put, improve it? It's great to realize that a goal becomes a sub-goal when it's been reached.

MY FOOD FOR THOUGHT ON AMBITIONS AND SUB-GOAL

AMBITION

The desire to be successful in your chosen field.
Ambition, requires a lot of renunciation and sacrifice.
If you are not motivated and single-minded,
you may never reach the goal.

2013

THE TARGET

Hitting a Target does not necessarily mean that you have used a weapon.

2015

FOCUS AND VISION

Focusing on the goal is most important of all - while Vision is needed to check that all conditions are in place to reach it.

GOAL

The closer you get to the Goal the more important the details become.

May 2019

ATTITUDES

2016

Without attitudes, I disregard the physical, and much would look different in our world.

It's probably not as if everybody has attitudes of the kind I'm thinking about, or more specifically said, conscious attitudes.

That is surely as it should be, but then it is also important that those with conscious attitudes stand up for them, and that may be more of a challenge.

"My attitude to that matter is". Dominant attitude: here it is about people with clear attitudes, at least in their own opinion, and they wish to express them.

Many certainly have attitudes that they seek to live up to in every way.

Those I think of do not always have to express their attitudes, they only have them, live up to them, and in view of that, they appear in the eyes of others as people with attitudes.

If you think about it, there are no limits to what attitudes you represent and observe with others.

Here I refer to seventeen Food For Thought which I hope can give you a more detailed understanding of my views on Attitudes:

MY FOOD FOR THOUGHT ON ATTITUDES

BLACK – WHITE ATTITUDE

You simplify your views to an either/or.

HOPELESS AND HOPEFUL

As Hopeless, you can see no way other than giving up- while as Hopeful you strive to reach the goal.

IMPERVIOUS AND INFLUENCE-ABLE

As Impervious, you steer straight forward without paying attention to anything - while as Influenced you consider other's ideas and thoughts.

TOLERANT AND INTOLERANT

As a Tolerant person you remain indulgent for the sake of domestic peace - while as an Intolerant person you stand for your opinions to highlight yourself.

2016

LOVING AND UNLOVING

As Loving, you turn the other cheek with a smile - while as Unloving you do everything to reject further dialogue.

EVIL AND GOOD

As Evil, you want to see another's pain and suffering - while as Good you do everything to make others feel better.

COMPASSIONATE AND INSENSITIVE
As a Compassionate person, you take an interest in another's situation with sympathy - while as Insensitive you have no interest in it.

CARESSING AND REPELLENT
As Caressing, you feel comfortable and want close contact - while as Repellent you clearly indicate the desire for physical distance.

ANGRY AND SOUR
As Angry you react with strong expressions - while as Sour, you are sad and not very talkative.

2016

FRIENDLY AND UNFRIENDLY
As Friendly, you slip easily into most environments - while as Unfriendly, you will be standing outside.

DOMINANT AND FLEXIBLE
As a Dominant, you stick to your point of view - while as Flexible you adapt to others.

MOODY AND HUMOROUS
As Moody you appear weak in a social context - while as Humorous you will be remembered as positive.

2016

NEGATIVE PERSONAL ATTITUDE
I feel pity for those who must step on others to keep themselves afloat.

March 2019

STRONG AND WEAK I
As Strong, you emphasize your Strengths - while if Weak you suppress them.

STRONG AND WEAK II
The Weakness of the Strong - may be the Strength of the Weak.

April 2019

ATTITUDE CHANGE
As long as the one-sided phrase: "What can I make of it?" is given first priority, no valuable progress is made.
"What can I contribute?", in a sensible balance with "What can I make of it?", is a better way forward.

February 2019

ATTITUDES
The most important thing is that you maintain your Attitudes if you are happy with them.

2019

OPENNESS

April 1994

In my opinion we humans are not very open.

Some might think they are, but they're not - deep down. That we are calculating in most of what we do - goes against openness.

We only find genuine openness in nature, where calculations don't form the basis for anything at all.

Notice for instance how flowers attract the bees. The petals willingly let go of the heart of the flower, to make room for the bee - that's genuine openness.

I have two valves - one main valve located deep inside is often closed - and the other - the outer one - controls the flow from the inner to the outer valve. I'm lucky to have the outer circuit.

To those who don't know me, I probably seem open - I'm not.

I think most of us have at least two valves. It's important, very important, that you can protect yourself like the fox, having several exits from your den.

Openness can turn back on itself. Tell all and you become vulnerable.

It's better to let openness come in doses - study the reaction. Is it real?

Uncertainty - doesn't it come from a lack of openness?

What's it like in the animal kingdom? I can't imagine a cow in a field holding something back to achieve something specific.

Although, does a dog which is begging show openness? Hardly - it has just learnt from experience that by begging it will achieve something.

It's probably not human nature to be open. Were we like that originally, and have we just learnt not to be that way?

Is there more openness in primitive societies? In my opinion it would be logical if it were so.

We live in a closed society, it is said. Does that term mean that we don't let others in or at least only to a very small degree?

If idleness is the root of all evil - could openness, then be the root of all good?

See to it that you don't become too open; it may be good to hold something back - just in case your openness is abused.

***

MY FOOD FOR THOUGHT ON OPENNESS

EXPOSURE

Is it only stupid people who expose themselves, or is it a symbol of security and honesty?

April 2020

LISTEN TO THE WORLD

Listen to the World. Digest what you hear,
make use of what you find valuable and make the best out of the situation.

June 2019

TRANSPARENCY AND UNCERTAINTY

Uncertainty is often the result of a lack of transparency.

2019

TRANSPARENCY AND NATURE

True Transparency can only be found in nature, it has no limitations. There are no restrictions on anything.

2017

INSPIRATION

July 1994

A strange word – where does it come from? The word that is? Latin, of course – explained as: empathy, inhaling, perception, enthusiasm, divine impulse. In my translation it is like receiving something.

Well, where do you get inspiration from? Are we all given inspiration or is it granted too only a select few?

Regardless, we all need inspiration from time to time; or don't we?

In my opinion, inspiration is something which you can, to a certain extent, create.

You can't just sit there and wait for the inspiration to come. You must, as for instance in marketing, conduct outreach surveys to achieve results. The orders don't just come strolling along on their own.

Inspiration to do what, or for what?

We're used to artists needing inspiration to perform; we've sort of grown up with that.

I heard the other day that Grieg composed some of his best works in a tiny cabin in Utne. He apparently found valuable inspiration there. I don't believe the inspiration just came to him, he probably sought it out, just there in those scenic surroundings. His composer's hut, the little house down by the water, a stone's throw from the main house, we've all heard about.

The Norwegian painter Thaulow's unique rendering of flowing water: inspiration?

He apparently spent a lot of time "on sight" in the cold. Inspiration costs.

Is inspiration synonymous with creativity? It's easy to say that something successful consists of 10% inspiration and 90 % perspiration.

Quite possibly, and in my case the perspiration percentage could be increased to 99.

Regardless, we must admit that inspiration is a necessary factor, that little or nothing can be created without inspiration but, once again, where does it come from?

For some, it perhaps comes in the form of a revelation: eureka. In this context I find it natural to bring in our inborn curiosity as an element. Not the normal kind of curiosity, where you stick your nose into other people's business, but the kind of curiosity which consists of wanting to know what's hidden around the next corner.

You appear with an open mind, you are receptive, nothing enters a closed hand, as we know.

It's like with a funnel; the wider the opening the more goes through. If you bare that in mind you can, in a way, gather the ingredients, or put differently, collect the seeds which will germinate.

Perhaps that is inspiration.

The best form of inspiration probably comes from other people. In this case it's not a question of blind worship of people with authority and power.

We're not all the same. There are people with a special-radiance and power who don't abuse it.

Why was he or she inspiring to talk to? Why was it an inspiring meeting?

If you let yourself drift along, let yourself get immersed in …?

Is it when that happens that you get inspiration?

All in all, I feel that life itself is the most important inspiration.

****

MY FOOD FOR THOUGHT ON INSPIRATION

INSPIRATION AND ASPIRATION

Inspiration to create something is an essential ingredient for Aspiration - which is the desire to attain or achieve something you do not have, or become something that you want to be.

INSPIRATION I

Life itself is the most important Inspiration.

1994

INSPIRATION II

You can't just sit there and wait for the Inspiration to come. For instance, in marketing you must conduct outreach surveys in order to achieve results. The orders don't normally just come strolling by on their own.

July 1994

INSPIRATION III

If You have an open mind, you're receptive; nothing enters a closed mind, as we know. It's like a funnel: the wider the opening the more goes through.

If you bear that in mind you can, in a way, collect the ingredients, or put differently, collect the seeds that germinate.

2023

STUBBORNNESS

May 2012

I won't immediately characterize stubbornness as a disease in line with what I believe extreme jealousy to be. Here as elsewhere there are many degrees and nuances.

The simple, well-known form of stubbornness, which everyone has and at times applies, is of a relatively innocent character.

In fact, it can be both humorous and charming and is part of everyone's daily life and relationships.

We can also skip lightly over the kind of stubbornness children use to attract attention. That's a gift of nature and a prerequisite for development. It's not in any way damaging but has, of course, a strong impact on the child's upbringing. If the cry is honoured repeatedly to achieve family peace, it suggests that you are doing the wrong thing; so it's clear here as elsewhere that you must find a balance. Maybe in the long run family peace is more important?

As we know, black and white is not always a workable alternative. Perhaps it seems the simplest, but it is in no way the most character building.

We can probably all agree on what has been said so far: you must add a bit of spice to everyday life in order to make things work.

It is worse when someone's stubbornness becomes a kind of obsession, turning towards the fanatical. Against all odds and common sense, and with a total lack of logic and sense of reality, a lot of people forge ahead without considering the turbulence they're causing when dealing with others who, within the given context, react normally and use these very senses to navigate through the waters of everyday life. It is especially bad for people with a strong sense of fairness. Everything turns upside down when normal values are set aside by such brutal and illogical means.

The result is unfortunately quite often a temporary break in communication or worse.

Total resignation is felt by the affected party, while the initiator, with his or her extreme variety of stubbornness, moves on through life as if nothing has happened.

You must ask yourself if it's possible for someone to be so removed from reality that they have no idea of what they've started. Or could it be that they feel that it's a means, with a bit of luck, to achieving changes in conditions, things, or situations?

Both are probably adequate reasons.

Wouldn't it be easy for those affected to think, oh well, this is so crazy that we'll just let it go, take it all with a smile and defuse the situation?

Those who recognize themselves will probably say that they have, of course, tried it that way, but that there are limits to how far you can stretch when the situation repeats itself several times in a row over a long period of time.

Those who have managed to read this far probably ask themselves if the writer of these words can refer to his own frightening examples of stubbornness, and I can assure you he can.

MY FOOD FOR THOUGHT ON STUBBORNNESS

STUBBORNNESS

Anyone who doesn't give up always finds a solution.
Maybe not the right one, but anyway. Any solution gives freedom.

May 2019

STUBBORNNESS I

The worst Stubbornness is that which for some becomes too great an obsession, a turn towards the fanatical.

2016

STUBBORNNESS II

Stubbornness can easily lead to communication breakdowns and worse.

2019

STUBBORNNESS III

Some use Stubbornness to change conditions, things, or situations.

2020

DEPENDENCE

December 2013

In some form or other we are, I believe, always and throughout all stages of life dependent on someone or something. From the time we see the light of day for the first time, we are dependent.

No sooner has the umbilical cord been cut, we are normally at the mercy of the person we have been dependent on throughout the entire pregnancy. The big difference is that now others can move in and help take over some responsibility for our further development.

Regardless, we are still at the mercy of and dependent on someone else.

No matter where in the world we happen to be born, and under whatever circumstances, rich or poor, those who think money makes one independent are terribly mistaken; we are always dependent.

Can you make yourself independent from dependence? Only by extreme manoeuvres I would think. But do you really want to?

Dependence is quite natural, has a completely natural place in your everyday life.

We are always learning something, whether it be part of your formal school education or not.

Also, when you get out into the real world after school, it is always a question of learning something.

The day you give up and says enough is enough, there's no point in learning anymore, that's really the beginning of the end.

Regardless of how you look at it, you are dependent on others to learn.

It is said that he or she is self-taught. The basis of being self-taught must start with something you have learnt and thus, if you look at it in isolation, it is probably more a case of indirectly building on the experiences of others, which reveals us dependent again.

Dependence as a challenge faces many people who for various reasons need others around them to exist.

I can imagine, even if it isn't part of my own experience, that most people in such a situation will do their utmost to become independent.

Unfortunately, certain situations often make this impossible; you are just, and always will be, dependent on others.

The above examples relate to human dependence. What about the more distant dependences, those most of us don't think about too much in our daily lives?

For those of us who are lucky enough to be growing up in the so-called modern world, it is natural for both clean water and electricity to always be present. We take it for granted and complain about the smallest inconvenience, caused by a power failure or having no water for a few hours when a pipe has sprung a leak. Here we have entered material dependence, and this comes in many guises. We, the spoiled ones, take too many things for granted; after all, we pay for them through our taxes, don't we?

On the screen, appeals are made to put aside a few kroner a month for those millions of people who don't know what clean water looks like, and who barely encounter electricity in their everyday lives. Some people must go along with these requests, or we wouldn't see such campaigns on TV.

There are pictures of children drinking water with which we wouldn't even mix cement, and they must walk for hours every day to get to water sources for these precious drops. Regardless of your social level, dependence exists.

We have also become totally dependent on mobiles and the internet, as well as an ocean of other gadgets, and we feel like the world is coming to an end when occasional irregularities occur with these. We obviously are happy to be dependent.

Indeed, we insist on it in our everyday lives, by always aspiring to the newest and latest gimmicks. This, of course, doesn't apply to everyone but clearly to most of us.

Another form of dependence, and one which can be more serious for the person or people concerned, is the dependence which can affect your health, or which often destroys family life. Here you must be careful, as I believe there are several factors playing a part. Each one must think about themselves and their own lives. Otherwise, within the extent of time and interest, everyone can choose to involve themselves in organizations they believe may have a positive influence when fighting dependence and abuse.

I have fortunately never got to know any form of what I, from lack of knowledge, lump together under the heading "drugs".

From the age of seventeen to twenty-three I smoked cigarettes. The reason I quit over night was that, throughout adolescence, I had a constant struggle with my tonsils. Finally, the day came when I was called in for an operation to have them removed. My innate fear of everything to do with hospitals and white coats spurred me into action. The hospital visit was cancelled, and my last cigarette extinguished.

The fear must have remained in my subconscious, however, because until the last couple of decades I have at times had very unpleasant experiences with tonsillitis but have never again smoked.

Alcohol is a different story. Despite a steady trickle of red wine throughout the years, from the time I first discovered this gift of Bacchus – during my two-year stay in Italy at the age of seventeen and eighteen – until today I can honestly say that there have been no negative side-effects. Since the first days of my youth, I have never had what one might call a hangover, or to my knowledge any other adverse effects. The volume has stayed steady and at the same level for the last fifty years.

When my daughters grew up, we constantly heard about tragedies happening due to the association with certain types of "substances". I believe I chose the easiest way out by making it clear to them that, regardless of how much I loved them, I would help them with anything else, but if they got involved with "drugs" they would be on their own.

I believed then and I still do, that this is something everyone must deal with on their own. When you have got into this vicious circle, you can only get out of it on your own. I am humble and tolerant when it comes to other points of view in this matter, but am happy that we, as a family, have been spared this - at least as far as I know.

Since I have never been a gambler, I also don't know anything about this dependence, except what I might read about the problems which may befall both families and people who are unable to moderate themselves in this context. Again, it's a question of your personal balance and control over the danger of becoming dependent. It seldom effects your health if a balance exists, but there is no doubt that many families have broken up as a result, and that related tragedies take place every day.

To use but not abuse, in other words to find the golden middle way in all of life's challenges, is what you ought to strive for; but never forget that you must also live the one and only life you have been given on earth to the full.

***

MY FOOD FOR THOUGHT ON DEPENDENCE

DEPENDENCE I

If you have a special attitude to another person,
you should expect that she or he has a special attitude to you.

June 2018

DEPENDENCE II

Is it not, in some way, a sense of security in the fact that we Depend on each other?

Oct 2019

DEPENDENT AND INDEPENDENT

It it not a defeat to be Dependent - as long as you do everything you can to become Independent of what makes life miserable.

2018

DEPENDENCE III

No matter where in the world we happen to be born, and under
whatever circumstances, are terribly mistaken;
we are always dependent.

2013

CONSCIENCE

January 2001

Let me point out straight away that this is a very sensitive subject.

Conscience is probably one of the most flexible concepts there are, as it always involves morals as well as judgement and feelings.

Everyone bases their conscience on their own judgement and ethics, thus emphasizing its flexibility. In my book "Thoughts", the first 51 days of 2001, I wrote among other things about conscience:

"I suppose conscience is something we are all concerned about. Whether it be good conscience or bad, it will always be there as part of our daily life. Then there is something about suppressing a bad conscience and the pleasant feeling you get from a good one. It may have to do with important things or just silly little things, but it is always on your conscience."

At that time, I meant it the way I wrote it, that everyone in one way or another is concerned about their conscience. Now, almost 12 years later, I've revised things a bit as you will see later, when I state that many seem not to have any conscience at all.

We have laws, of course, which, in our democracies at least, are meant to be guidelines for how we are to behave in practically all situations. They are there for our own good according to those who have written them, but even though this is largely correct, I think most of us feel that we are swamped with laws and regulations and that many of them can only be understood by a selected few.

Everyday rules and regulations are fine, for example those concerning traffic. Here it's a question of saving lives and reducing damages.

Every one of us decides how the state's rules are to be followed based on judgement and conscience.

After many years' experiences of driving in Spain, my judgement is usually based on the theory that, despite the speed limit of 40, most people drive between 60 and 80. The motorway limit of 120 means a minimum of 130 and is often closer to 150, with many exceptions over 170.

The stop signs mean, to a lot of people, just go if the road is free.

Especially for most of the locals in small towns, one-way signs mean: "Just drive if no one is coming against you and you can get quickly to your destination".

A widespread sport for those who normally drive at 150 on the motorway, is to see how close you can get to the car in front without making physical contact.

I must admit though that a greater respect is shown at pedestrian crossings.

It's no longer a sport to see how close to the pedestrians one can get without hitting them.

Most things are improving after all.

All examples seem to be based more on judgement than conscience.

According to their own judgement everyone acts correctly.

So far it was all about judgement, but where does conscience enter the picture?

Lots of people probably have no conscience at all, so they just drive around in their own world. While many probably have a conscience but it's buried and doesn't surface until an accident has happened and it's too late.

For whom or for what should you have a conscience in traffic?

I don't want to be seen as a saint in this case, because I'm not, but let's look at drinking and driving for instance. In this I'm quite consistent and I can confirm that, since I was 20 years old and until I first came to Spain about 15 or 20 years ago, there was seldom, if ever, a question of having a single glass when the car was my mode of transport. Things did change to a certain degree upon arriving in Spain, where a glass or two with meals followed by a brandy with one's coffee, didn't stop anyone from driving home.

Having a morning coffee in the local bar, you often saw the local police with their *carajillos* (coffee with a dash of brandy) at the start of their working day. I think I became quite conscious of what I was doing, drove more carefully and did not suffer from a bad conscience, but I would be telling a lie if I said that, at the beginning and until the late nineties when I was here only on sporadic visits, I kept to my Norwegian habits.

Gradually, as the rules were sharpened here as well, with regular controls, everything changed. Today the combination of drinking and driving has become unthinkable for most people and that's as it should be.

I don't know whether it has to do with my conscience or my moral responsibility not to hurt others, but if it has to do with both so much better, I now choose total abstinence when driving.

Perhaps most of it does have to do with the tiny good or bad consciences. The big ones are probably so overwhelming that if you have a conscience to begin with, you try "the ostrich game". To put your head in the sand and pretend you aren't there.

Has anyone tried to examine or count their good and bad consciences? I wonder if anyone could come up with some sort of norm, showing the percentage which would bring you within acceptable limits.

It would probably be too complicated, however, and your conscience shouldn't be left to others, as it is clearly among your most personal possessions.

I have at least one bad conscience, which I don't want to share with anyone until one day I've left it behind.

The more I think about all this, the more I must admit that I too, to some extent, participate in "the ostrich game" in this context.

Conscience, judgement, and morals belong together. Of all the proverbs I've seen about the conscience, this Persian one is the finest:

"The zest for life comes from a clear conscience".

MY FOOD FOR THOUGHT ON CONSCIENCE

CONSCIENCE I

Nothing is better than the feeling of a clear Conscience.

CONSCIENCE II

If you believe you made a bad decision that had an adverse effect on someone or something, then your "Conscience" is not clear on that act. However, it can be clear on other decisions you have made.

November 2012

CONSCIENCE III

Whether it concerns a good or bad Conscience, it is always with us as part of our daily life.

2023

GOOD AND BAD CONSCIENCE

Everyone is acquainted with both Good and Bad Conscience - while the degree of the good or the bad is essential to our well-being.

EXPERIENCE

October 2013

There is something pretentious about the word experience. "Experience suggests that".

As a general expression, you normally let it pass without closer reflection, but if it is connected to serious speeches presented by people in authority, you ought to listen carefully.

Where would we be without the lessons experience teaches?

Wouldn't we just be repeating our actions, whether the repetitions are justified or not?

How often would we be correct in our repetition? In our everyday life we are not consciously aware of the way we use our experience. For most of us, we automatically draw our own conclusions. We base our actions on our experiences and subconsciously make minor or major adjustments.

As a result, it is one of the main factors which help us develop throughout our entire life. It would be very sad if, at some point, we told ourselves that that's sufficient experience, let's flick the switch.

In a way it would be the same as putting your hands in the air saying, I've got nothing more to learn, there's no point to the learning process.

Those people who consciously acquire knowledge until the very end are the happiest.

It is of course also true that theoretical knowledge builds experience, though not immediately in a practical way.

Is there also something called spiritual experience, which complements practical experience?

Through schools and universities, you get an academic education. The experiences you have gained because of your studies are, of course, both valuable and necessary, you hope, when it comes to applying for a job. But even when your career choice isn't of a practical kind, but of a more academic type, the question of experience is always raised.

You stand there with your exam results and are treated the same as all the other applicants. Regardless of who gets the position and the criteria used, you can ask yourself who should cover the costs to get the experience, which must be gained to do the job properly.

It's most likely the employer who must invest to benefit fully from their employees' education, and that is probably as it should be. Naturally enough, you can't be equipped for the task you are given before you have gained the right experience.

A different situation involves education of a more basic character, which needs to be combined with business practice within a chosen profession. This combination of schooling and practical experience is, in my opinion, by far the best when it comes to career choices. I hope it still exists in some form or other.

When I started working at the end of the fifties, we had several apprentices employed in our firm. They were to reach their journeyman or trade examinations.

They were normally employed in the service department, had apprenticeship contracts and, if I remember correctly, were given two days a week off to attend the vocational school to get a theoretical education.

As far as I can understand, this arrangement has been replaced with other versions, but I'm not up to date on this.

The question is if the apprenticeship scheme, in a more modernized form than the one we had back then, wouldn't be better and more interesting for many of those who feel the need to get into a craft early on, rather than fight their way through a higher theoretical education in which they have little or no interest.

I have heard that the apprenticeship scheme is practised successfully in Switzerland, for instance, and that in England there are constant references to the fact that more apprenticeships ought to be created.

I take this as a sign that this form of education is still considered the best when it comes to practical training.

I greatly believe in a working environment involving a combination of theoretical and practical training.

I have often heard said, "If only others could learn from our hard-earned experiences, how much better everything would be."That way of thinking is both short-sighted and meaningless in my opinion. You must be the master of your own experiences; I'll go so far as to say that it is only through your own experiences that you can progress. Here I exclude obvious well-accepted experience based on investigation and science. Such experience belongs to all theoretical education on all levels, and automatically provides a positive benefit in most cases.

In this context knowledge can be drawn from other people's experiences.

Not that you ought to believe that all experience is worthwhile; and I don't think anyone does. Everyone has, in one form or other, suffered a bad experience.

The conclusion is that it isn't important if your experiences are good or bad, if you learn from them.

Bad experiences don't trigger repeats, while the good ones ought to do so.

I believe it would be good for us all to focus more on the value of experience.

Think about the experiences you have benefited from in life, especially where you believe they have been important for your development. Then become more conscious of them.

Most of us are, I believe, equipped with a good or not so good ability to suppress bad experiences. I call this ability a safety valve. We can't keep filling up with too much negativity, especially as regards the bad experiences we suffer from at times.

We ought to suppress some memories of them, when we feel that it's necessary, to maintain an acceptable balance.

I believe that the best experiences that have contributed to my development, I gained during my time at school in Italy in the late nineteen fifties.

MY FOOD FOR THOUGHT ON EXPERIENCE

EXPERIENCE I

Bad Experiences do not trigger repetition - while the good ones should inspire them.
It may be good for all of us to focus more on Experiences.
Think about what Experiences you have had throughout your life, of the kind that you think have been of importance to your development, then raise your awareness of them.

October 2013

EXPERIENCE II

Not all Experiences are of the good kind, but they are part of our lives and thus help shape our personality.

Dec. 2019

EXPERIENCE AND KNOWLEDGE

Experience is something you gain over time
- while Knowledge is a result of Experience.

EXPERIENCES

It's unwise to underestimate Experiences.

2013

COMMUNICATION AND THE VOICE

April 2013

Communication is largely what you want it to be.

As the communication I'm thinking of here is verbal, I have in this reflection, included part of my Reflection "The Voice" from 1995.

In my opinion, the best definition of communication is: "the process which has the unit of thought as its aim" from Wikipedia.

There are many definitions, of course. Just think of how versatile communication is, regardless of context.

As mentioned before, I'm married to Marianne who is Swiss. In May we will have been married for fifteen years and while my Spanish is quite limited, she speaks it fluently. I don't speak French, which is her mother tongue. We have always, between the two of us communicated in English.

Even though I'm a British citizen, I've been based in Norway all my life and have thus only my Norwegian school English as a starting point; and there wasn't a lot of regular school.

Regardless, it's a great combination. Even though you normally become more tolerant and understanding towards your marital partner as the years go by, very few believe me when I say that in these nearly fifteen years we have never come close to having what I would describe as an argument. The answer lies, among other things, in having as a safety net the fact that you are not communicating in your mother tongue. "I must have misunderstood what you meant".

This immediately shows your tolerance, but also affords the better half the possibility of smoothing things over by saying: "Yes, I realise that you must have misunderstood. What I really meant was..."

Is this communication? Regardless, no one must feel defeated or lose their pride; aren't we lucky?

I hope no one takes me too literally in this; it's probably not all that simple.

I don't think a poor foundation can be fixed this way. Communication has, as mentioned, an infinite range. The voice itself used for verbal expression is decidedly the most convenient form of communication, and it is here, in my opinion, that the perfection of the voice shows itself.

A word, a sentence, with different intonations, is interpreted differently. This happens when you can't see the person you are talking to. Joy, sorrow, expectation, and questions, all expressed in a combination of phraseology and intonation.

The intonation expresses, often better than the words themselves, a particular state of mind.

In connection with an earlier reflection – the one that I wrote about the smile, I included both the voice and the eyes, because I wondered whether the smile could stand on its own, or if it had to be seen together with, for instance, the voice and the eyes.

In that context I felt that it was natural to ask the question; but regarding the voice, it can hold its own and it does so quite often.

Not least every time you are calling someone. Depending on the nature of the conversation, your voice changes intuitively according to the messages you want to convey.

Answer words, expressed in different ways, can give you anything from the strongest fear to the purest joy.

The divine instrument can play on a never-ending number of strings.

Even animals are very sensitive to this instrument. No one believes that they understand the language that's being spoken to them. No, they react, of course, to the voice as such.

We are perhaps not conscious enough of the way we use our voice, or is that precisely what we are? Shouldn't you always, and especially when speaking on the telephone, consciously think about how your voice is interpreted by the person you are talking to? It becomes especially important perhaps, when it has to do with people who are closely connected to one another, and where subtle nuances are significant.

The further you are apart, geographically speaking, the more importance I feel you should give to this.

The voice is also a significant weapon and very versatile when used as such.

The funny thing is that precisely when used as a weapon, the voice is perhaps the best of its kind; but, unlike others, it can have its greatest effect when not being used.

Is there something called "silence to death"?

The voice can both love and hate, but we mustn't let

our-selves be misled into thinking that it operates on its own.

Some people speak without thinking, of course, but that's not what I mean.

No, the voice will forever remain an instrument and, as such, is controlled by the brain.

My personal experience with communication over the years has been all enveloping, in the sense that I, as an employer, had close contact with employees on all levels and of both sexes. Only rarely, as far as I recall, was it necessary to admit to a failure of communication.

I didn't always live up to the policy of my firm. Each employee should have the full right to know as much about the running of the firm, so that even if they didn't always agree with its decisions and objectives, they should, if interested, be able to understand the motives behind them.

It obviously didn't sound quite like that in the company policy, which I wrote at the time, but this part has unfortunately been lost somewhere along the way.

These days such ideals may sound totally misplaced in the business world, and attitudes like these probably find little acceptance in today's personnel management.

In a family context, my experiences as regards to communication, especially in my younger days, was a little different. I was at times accused of being a coward when I didn't enter what were, in my opinion, one-way arguments, the outcome of which had already been decided before any communication had begun.

There's something in the saying that "where there is nothing, even the emperor has lost his rights".

Fortunately, these situations were few and far between, but they have stuck in my mind.

Distortion of the truth or a totally one-sided attitude make communication difficult, if not impossible, and the same goes for unwarranted accusations. Desperation builds and that's when you see compromise or giving up as the only solution.

Many will probably draw the conclusion here that I can't have been easy to get on with, and I can sympathise with this view. I don't know if my personal experiences have left scars that are too deep, but the wounds have not been easy to heal.

I hasten to say that I have an excellent relationship with most people I know, so in that context I'm talking about water under the bridge.

If a partnership is based on a solid foundation, it should, in most cases, be possible to come to an agreement through communication based on compromise.

MY FOOD FOR THOUGHT ON COMMUNICATION AND THE VOICE

COMMUNICATION I

The ideal form of Communication is the one that even those without preconception can use and enjoy.

1989

COMMUNICATION II

You improve understanding by recognizing that details and shades are needed for a balanced Communication.

October 2013

COMMUNICATION – BELIEFS

One of the reasons why Communication becomes complicated is that everyone is right based on their beliefs.

2018

TALKATIVE AND LISTENER

As Talkative everything goes out while little comes in.
As a good Listener everything comes in,
while only that which is of value to the person stays there.
The combination of being Talkative and at the same time a good Listener is an art form.

Sept. 2019

COMPROMISE

March 2013

Everyone has a clear idea of what the word compromise means.

Making compromises in our daily lives is quite common for most of us. We don't normally give it much thought, nor do we look at compromise as being a sacrifice. I give a little here, the other party gives a little there, then we make a compromise having given way equally, without either party having got things exactly his or her way.

Is it really that simple?

I would like to believe that the simplest form of compromise is the one that produces no consequences other than personal sacrifice. By that I mean that no other than the parties involved should personally suffer from the cost the compromise demanded. That can be serious enough, but in any case, you have full control over the consequences and can judge for yourself whether others will be harmed.

It becomes more complicated when someone enters an act of compromise on behalf of others. Here, the consequences can be very serious, so the person who has authorised the compromise to be entered into, should have done thorough research about the consequences this could have.

It can be even more challenging with compromises that are made, where the consequences can be of a completely different dimension. For example, when countries make trade agreements between themselves, or things like that. In such cases, it is usually delegations from the parties who negotiate until a compromise is reached. The consequences will probably not normally be directly personal, but may have other far-reaching consequences.

The above mentioned consequences of compromises are fortunately not something you normally think about in the daily life and hopefully it is the case that some of us enter compromises without thinking too much about the consequences, and that is good.

It is precisely those small daily compromises that you should get used to making to maintain balance in life, as they have an inestimable importance for your own self-satisfaction.

When travelling around, you find places where, in certain situations, all trade is based on bargaining. The seller starts with prices that are sky-high, the idea being that these will be brought down to a level, which both parties are happy with. This is also a form of compromise, but in my opinion a somewhat misguided one. Here there is no equal distribution of giving. The seller's contribution, the reduction in price, has been put in as a calculating factor. He knows where to draw the line, in other words, the lowest acceptable price, which still gives him a reasonable profit. The buyer on his or her part should also be aware of the situation and close the deal only if he or she finds the price acceptable.

Am I in the wrong here?

I'm far from happy with this procedure, regardless of the cultures practising it.

If I must compromise, however, perhaps it isn't so bad after all?

Is it only because I'm generally not happy with this type of procedure that I don't like it?

Many of you probably feel that this is just the right form for trade, as here one can argue and negotiate and influence the outcome.

At least that's what you think, but those of us who are a bit wiser, know that it, the price that is, has already been decided beforehand: it's the seller who decides.

Those who share my attitude normally pay too much, to the seller's delight. In other words, you ought to stay away from this type of trade if you aren't familiar with this form of bargaining. Some love it. They feel great when they can let loose in this type of situation and that's good for them.

Now, let's get back to compromise, which is the result of negotiations where none of the parties gets things 100% as they want them, but are still happy.

I mentioned that there is no sacrifice in this form of compromise, and I believe that; but let's look at the kind of compromise where the distribution of benefits is in no way equal, where one of the parties feels that he or she has given a lot more than the other one but goes along with it in any case. This can be tiring after a while.

That it happens occasionally can't be avoided and it usually works both ways, but when the scales keep tipping in one direction it can become difficult.

My original name, before I was given the surname, Manus, by my stepfather Max on my eighteenth birthday, was George Hans Bernardes. George after my English father and Hans because my mother felt there should be something Norwegian in my name. (Hans isn't just the name of a king of Norway from 1483 to 1513, like George in England, but also a family name from Ulvik in Hardanger.)

Here there was probably also a compromise, as I was given the name Manus, but was never adopted.

MY FOOD FOR THOUGHT ON COMPROMISE

COMPROMISE I

Compromise is probably one of the most important words we have, apart from love.

2017

COMPROMISE II

If the parties are not completely out of balance, Compromise should be possible to reach.

2013

COMPROMISE III

The ability to compromise is something we must all learn,
but whatever you do, don't let it become a permanent state.

April 2019

COMPROMISE AND HONESTY

There is no point in Compromising Honesty,
as it's only a question of time before disclosure comes with unexpected and usually unpleasant consequences.

April 2014

TRUTH

March 2014

When you hear the expression, "The truth is…", then be on the alert.

In my opinion, anyone using this phrase lacks an understanding of reality.

A person using the expression, "The truth is…" without immediately adding "in my opinion", is lacking any form of credibility.

What is true and isn't, is, unfortunately a stretchy concept for many.

The expression, "the Truth is…" is just as hopeless as described in an earlier reflection, which was called "To be honest".

It's easy to mix the use of the word's truth and honesty. In many ways, they go together, but of course do not.

I never heard anyone say, "This is my honest truth". If that was the case, the reason must have been to underline the truth.

Think about it. In this case, first you emphasize your "honesty", underlining you're general honest. Second you make the mistake of telling the "Truth" unconditionally. The truth for whom?

Typically, this case demands an amendment such as, for example, "Subjectively, this is my honest truth".

Anyhow, in my opinion, there is, nevertheless, a big difference between the words truth and honesty.

The "truth", even when being treated sloppily by many,

is of course not stretchy, it's black or white. Either it is true or it's not true, or it's false.

The closest example I can come up with to put this concept of "the incorrect truth and the correct truth" into a more understandable light, is to have a look at the media.

Probably today's most dominating media outlet for news and information, is the TV.

Of course, there is also the written press together with a lot of social media, which is increasingly used in conjunction with modern technology.

This however is much too comprehensive to deal with in a little reflection like this.

I stick to the TV and imagine that there are more than 30000 television stations in the world.

No use to touch the countries working with only state-controlled TV. In my opinion, in such cases the "correct truth" never reaches the population.

With tens of thousands of channels, it's obvious there are equally many influencing possibilities.

In Europe alone there are more than 11000 channels available. It's not as if they all transmit news, of course, or that they perform in any way a conscious influence on us viewers; but within all genera they focus on "truth". Some of them like to be the carrier of "truth", and others claim they are the one presenting the "correct truth".

I will limit myself to one example which I, in turn, think is quite engraving. There is no reason to hide which channel I'm referring to – I mean CNN; a news channel claiming to be the largest in the world.

Here I got to know by one of the top journalists, in an advertisement to promote the channel, that she had a new twist on her reporting, she was going to tell the "truth". Important for us listeners to know.

As far as I remember, after continuous repetition, it was taken off after a few months; so obviously someone must have discovered the blunder.

From my perspective, the essential thing when dealing with the "truth", is that you see it in conjunction with objectivity.

The person or people claiming that their channel stands for the "correct truth" must, if they look for credibility, emphasize that they present their information based on their own objective review. It means that they have judged the "truth" of the information in question from the outside, put themselves in a position to objectively look at all sides of the case.

One thing is the objective attitude towards the "truth", but do you have time to go into all the details, and is it re-ally that important?

The news comes first they say; and of course it's important to be the first.

Correctness, meaning the "truth". Yes, of course, it's important that what's presented is "true", but at the same time it's even more important that the number of viewers are retained and increased?

This happens only if the public feel that the channel in

question is delivering.

The fact that an enormous number of channels are available must not be forgotten. Many of them are transmitting content where the "truth" is not looked upon as being important. Could it be that all channels on TV have their own norms about the "truth", and that they are based on the owner's assumptions, attitude, and economic interests?

What happens to the "truth" in the middle of all this? So-called "authentic reporting" must also be mentioned.

"Authentic" defines something as genuine, original or something having its own character. Nothing is mentioned about "truth", and that's maybe not necessary?

Maybe it's easier for the TV companies to identify them- selves with an "authentic" form of "truth". Is that "truth" more tolerant than the general "truth"?

The expression: "The truth may be in between" may for many seem logical; but does anyone believe that if you take news from RT (Russian Television) and CNN and divide them in two, you get the correct "truth"?

Maybe an extreme example as I have understood that the RT channel is state controlled.

Could there be anything in the saying, "the origin of truth, the source, can be the truth's worst enemy"?

Unfortunately, nothing in the world can be ideal, so maybe we must accept the "truth" we are faced with in daily life and use our common sense.

MY FOOD FOR THOUGHT ON TRUTH

TRUTH AND UNTRUTH

What is despairing is that Truth for someone is Untruth to others. The golden middle way cannot be used in terms of Truth and Untruth.

2018

TRUTH AND LIES I

Whoever possesses Truth is rich
- while the Liar for all time will remain poor.

TRUTH AND LIES II

If the claim that everyone is right based on their beliefs is correct, and who can contradict that, there will be an infinite spectrum between the extremes of Truth and Lies.
The same will apply to information from so-called reliable sources.

2018

"THE TRUTH IS..."

Truths are correct for the person who uses the phrase: "The truth is...", but will always reflect on his or her prerequisites.

December 2018

HONESTY

September 2012

It is high time I grabbed hold of "honesty" and finally come to terms with this, for me, painful subject.

Ever since I started working, I have been immensely irritated by the expression, "to be honest", or its other variation, "in all honesty". Not only has it irritated me all these years, but at times it also made me furious, because I cannot imagine a more idiotic expression, within the contexts in which it is normally used.

How can you trust someone using these kinds of phrases? What the person in question is saying is that, normally I'm a totally dishonest person, but in this situation, I will make an exception, namely, to be honest. Stuff and nonsense.

Now, of course, there will be many reading this who, if being honest with themselves, will realize that they themselves use this expression. To you I have only got one thing to say, and that is: stop using it this very instant.

Next time you hear someone expressing him- or herself, listen carefully. You will be surprised at how much dishonesty you will observe.

Of course, you can say that this does not mean much within the greater context, as it is only a matter of an expression. There's no way I personally can take that attitude.

While I am on the subject, it feels natural to add the expression: "Truth be told". What on earth is the meaning of that? Should the truth not normally be in the forefront? Does it mean that you are not normally trustworthy, not expressing the truth? Is the truth to be saved and only brought forth at special events or occasions?

In my opinion, if that's the case, the world has become unhinged.

A typical old-man's expression you might say. Very well, but if that is your attitude it means that you are either indifferent to the above-mentioned approach, or you accept it.

Don't forget that another generation is coming after us. What are they going to believe and think if we don't give them guidelines?

Again, the excuse of many will be these are just clichés. I regret this attitude is too prolific in our daily communication. Most of us, I think, will fight for the freedom of speech and the right to express ourselves. In the spirit of democracy, we want it that way.

Some Danes have made cartoons offending the Prophet Mohammed, while a video recently produced also seems to offend those who worship the Prophet, and who have him as their guide in life. Retaliations, riots, and killings have been the result of it all.

We live in a world which allows us insight into whatever we want. The whole world is open to us if we are interested. How many religions and communities do we have on this planet? Furthermore, how many sects and special varieties do we have who represent different opinions of how life should be lived and what it should consist of.

At the end of the day, the questions will be and have

probably always been the same: who is the strongest, who will win and what means will they use to win, or at least advance in the hierarchy of preferred religions and their splinter groups?

However, "being honest", I think that every one of us should be able to live as we wish and make the best out of our life on earth, based on our own assumptions, but that is when I am "being honest".

This last statement has probably got its weaknesses. What would I mean in this context if I were to be dishonest? If I had skipped the first "to be honest", I think my basic attitude would be crystal clear.

Summary: I think that every one of us should be able to live as we wish and make the best out of our life on earth, based on our own assumptions.

***

MY FOOD FOR THOUGHT ON HONESTY

HONEST FEELINGS

Respect peoples' Honest Feelings - and treat them gently.

HONESTY I

Honesty has no competitors.

HONESTY II

Honesty is also not to be despised.
Suspicion and jealousy are poison and can be hidden dangers on the road of life. If you make Honesty part of your daily agenda, as well as a good portion of tolerance and respect for one another, many of life's sharp edges can be rounded.

From a wedding speech in 2005

HONESTY AND LIES

If you Focus on Honesty and gives it full support - Lies will retreat without a fight.

PATIENCE

January 2019

"I'll be right there".

It usually starts with an agreement that something is going to take place at a specific time, but which for unknown reasons is being delayed.

Both parties are ready, and a time is confirmed between themselves. Then, for some reason, one of them got hindered and thereby delayed. The one who, according to the agreement, expects that the thing that should happen will happen, in other words the one not causing the delay, will normally, from the time the agreement was made, start the countdown by showing patience.

This is where each of us shows our quality of being patient or lacking it. What makes most of us tend to lose patience at some point, is when a delay that is more than expected takes place.

Is it the time we lose that we see as valuable, or is it the shortcoming of expectations? The agreement is made, and the expectations are thereby unconsciously built up, only for them to be pushed forward in time.

Is patience a human phenomenon? Animals, especially domestic animals such as dogs and cats, do not seem to have the same problems with patience as we humans, at least not the question of patience that has to do with time. Is it because their assessment of time is different from ours, or that their instinctual expectations are different?

Dogs, which I have most experience with, especially

English setters, certainly do not lack expectations. They, who otherwise appear to be devoid of this property in their daily lives are quite clear when the hunting season is on. Then they reveal expectations to the fullest. Whether it's experience because they are used for hunting or if it's inherited instincts, I do not know; but I have many examples that show that they possess strong expectations and that there is no way they can control their impatience.

When I think about it, it's far from correct that dogs appear to be devoid of patience in their daily lives. Just look at the tail movement of the dog when you retrieve the dog lead, or when you are on your way to performing another of the dog's daily positive routines. The dog's patience does not turn into irritation if the action fails to take place; but, when that happens, you can clearly read the disappointment resulting from the failed expectations, in the dog's body language.

Not all types of patience have something to do with time.

Take, for example, the patience that is related to things where you compromise daily. Here too patience can be put to the test. Different kinds of bad habits, or repetitive patterns of action that you are not totally excited in others, are not always solved by allowing it to lead to criticism, which then becomes the subject of hurtful discussions. No, instead you allow tolerance to lubricate your patience.

This model can often be used successfully over short periods of time, but if you compromise by using tolerance and patience over too long a time, it can harm your health.

Another thing is that the possible expectation that the cause of the bad habit, or the repeated annoying pattern of action, will disappear by itself, is something you will rarely or never experience.

If we could all be a little more conscious when it comes to giving others reasons to put their patience to the test, much in everyday life would be easier.

MY FOOD FOR THOUGHT ON PATIENCE

PATIENCE II

Unfortunately, Patience is often exploited and rarely gets any other thanks than the good feeling of helping others.

PATIENT AND IMPATIENT

As Patient you wait with a smile - while as Impatient you get upset and stressed.

January 2019

PATIENCE AND EXPECTATIONS I

Patience becomes less, the greater the Expectations you have.

January 2019

PATIENCE AND EXPECTATIONS II

If we could all be a little more conscious about not giving other reasons to test their Patience, much in everyday life would be better.

January 2019

FEELINGS

April 2014

Everything in life must have to do with feelings. Without feelings mankind wouldn't have survived.

According to the encyclopaedia, feelings are described among other things as emotions and affections. Emotions involve various complex mind reactions, such as pleasure, sympathy, compassion, sorrow, disgust, etc.

This might become clearer if you use the example that it's impossible to be happy on request. Feelings must be real and immediate.

I feel that most of us have clear opinions about feelings. We become acquainted with feelings from a very early age. Children show their feelings unconsciously and without reserve; they are wonderfully innocent.

Real feelings must be separated from false ones. All of us probably feel intuitively what this means.

Here – as elsewhere in life –, priority must be given to honesty, as then all of this becomes a lot easier. Apart from a few exceptions, which I don't see any reason to get into, there is no point in compromising, as it's only a question of time before you are exposed, usually followed by unexpected and unpleasant consequences.

What would love be without feelings? The answer speaks for itself, doesn't it?

Real love can't exist without feelings, and that means that love based on false feelings hasn't got anything to do with love.

Strong opinion?

Absolutely, but as always it's just my opinion, as I'm convinced that there are others who would put it differently. To each his own.

To show and express feelings is something very personal. In most cases, the ability to do so goes deep, but that doesn't mean that those who outwardly have difficulty showing or expressing their feelings lack the ability to do so; the opposite is often the case.

Trust and security may often be what's needed for introverts to open up their feelings.

Regardless, everything to do with feelings is a delicate balancing act, which, if it doesn't happen naturally, is also not right.

To have feelings for someone is not the same as to feel for someone.

Compassion is a certain type of feeling, which doesn't directly affect yourself. It's a feeling you give to others in the form of sympathy and understanding.

If you are compassionate with others, the good feeling returns like a boomerang, which makes it feel especially good.

It's well-known that animals have senses which we humans don't share. It's said that they can feel earthquakes, storms, and other natural phenomena before they happen. Because we humans feel that we have physical control over most things, we set aside the fact that we also possess senses of a special character. In my opinion, there's no doubt that such senses were more prominent in pre-historic times, but, as evolution changed us into more "modern" beings, the need for these ancient senses diminished.

Nevertheless, there are still some remaining capabilities from the days when we were more "animal-like". Not everyone is aware of this, and why should they be, as the need for them is no longer obvious in your everyday life?

The expression "I feel it in my bones" is one that fits into this category, and which sounds perhaps very grandma-like.

Regardless, if you leave the door of your scepticism just slightly ajar, this isn't so far-fetched.

Good feelings, mixed feelings, or bad feelings. I think most of us can distinguish between these three types of feelings, and, more precisely, identify which one of the three applies in any situation. Why? Because you have a feeling about it, that's all.

Likewise, I believe it's easy for most of us to describe others as either not having any feelings, or being cold or warm when it comes to showing them.

It becomes more difficult when it comes to describing yourself. I'm not quite clear on what it means "to listen to music with feeling". It probably doesn't refer to the music itself having feelings, or does it? No, it's probably that your feelings become engaged when you listen to certain pieces of music which makes you feel good.

Up until now it has all been about feelings and the incredible sense they represent; if feelings can be characterized as a sense, that is.

What then about the physical side of things, the one which has to do with losing your feeling? The term is too broad to broach here, but in my opinion, there is no doubt that those who, in some form or other, have experienced this have their own special challenges to deal with. Perhaps it's often because in such situations you choose to keep your feelings to yourself.

Don't you also feel that there's some truth in this?

After committing this reflection to paper, I seemed to remember that in two previous reflections I had come close to dealing with feelings, and, right enough, when I went through them, I found one about "sensitive hands" from April 1994, and one on "sensitivity" from May of the same year.

I must admit that it would be too much for me at this point to check if there are any contradictions or repetitions present, but there must presumably be some sort of connection between sensitive hands, sensitivity, and feelings.

Perhaps someone has sufficient energy to look?

***

MY FOOD FOR THOUGH ON FEELINGS

FEELING FOR OR WITH

The Feelings you have For someone are very different from Feelings of being With someone.

April 2014

CONFIDENCE AND SECURITY

Confidence and Security are factors that make it possible to open up for emotions.

April 2014

COMPASSION

Compassion is the type of Feeling you give to others in the form of sympathy and understanding. If given naturally to someone else, the good Feeling returns like a boomerang, which makes it Feel especially good.

2014

TO SHOW EMOTION

To Show Emotion is a spontaneous unconscious form of expression that you must respect.

May 2019

SELF-ASSESSMENT AND SELF-CRITICISM

December 2018

Could it be possible that this topic came to me completely by itself, or was it triggered by something very special?

It doesn't matter. It's a typical example of something that has been lying and smouldering, which the subconscious has quietly worked with over time.

Tolerance has, of course, been put to the test for a long time, and all forms of compromise available have also been nurtured.

If I don't immediately mention that a case or an opinion at least has two sides, or parties, and that I am conscious about it, anyone could say that this isn't an objective opinion, but a clearly subjective assessment.

Admittedly, when I feel pressured, I am not the easiest, but at least I have a willingness to try to build bridges.

The way we look at ourselves or judge ourselves may vary quite considerably, as we are all different.

Nevertheless, the main feature is that we generally add better qualities to ourselves; that we think we are a little better than we really are, and that we have a clearer view of most things than most others.

Here it sprinkles with the fertilizer for self-preservation. What about self-criticism? Clearly, most of us think we are self-critical. We generally don't like to be criticized, but if we criticize ourselves, it stays only between ourselves and our own conscience.

No one gets to know where we really stand. There's a

lot of good protection in that, and you are not so easily exposed. Many find themselves in such a world. In that way, they shield themselves from the outside, believing that everything is fine and green, and for them it is so. They often remain in their own world, find their place in the hierarchy and function perfectly in the whole.

There are areas where I think it's appropriate to exercise some self-criticism, however, and that is related to behaviour in everyday life. Ask yourself if you are a person who usually takes others into account?

Think about it carefully. It's not a matter of covering a big field. From the moment you start the day to when you go to bed, you encounter an infinity of situations where you deliberately or unconsciously leave an imprint of your personality.

You are judged by others based on your actions and behaviour. If your attitude is that you do not care, then you can't expect anything but general negativity towards your personality.

In this context, it's amazing how important the real smile is.

A smile costs nothing but gives so much. Yes, I claim that it requires very little from your side to be perceived as a considerate human being.

Not that you should in any way expect someone to give you this in writing; but the most valuable gain you're guaranteed to get is your own good feeling of knowing that you are generally a considerate human being.

Now, don't let this go to your head. You will have many negative feelings if you're not perceived as how you want to be; but it's not your problem if you are otherwise satisfied with the sincere attempts you have made to act more considerately in daily life.

MY FOOD FOR THOUGHT ON SELF-ASSESSMENT AND SELF-CRITICISM

SELF-ASSESSMENT-SELF-CRITICISM

The best way to become a better person is honest Self-Assessment checked through Self-Criticism.

December 2010

SELF-CONSCIOUSNESS

Being Self-Conscious is in no way the same as being egoistic.

May 2019

SELF-CONSCIOUS

None of us can help being the way we are, but it probably becomes easier, in many contexts, if we are a little more self-conscious.

SELF - PRESERVATION

In general, we believe we have better qualities than we have, that we are a little bit better than we are, and that we have a clearer view than most others. "The older we get the better we are."

December 2018

PRIDE

May 2014

"It's nothing to be proud of", or the opposite, "I'm proud of you", or: "You can be proud of that", are expressions you pay attention to, particularly if they come from someone with authority in one area or another and applies to yourself.

It's something about being careful before contacting someone with the expression, "It's nothing to be proud of". You should in advance have a thoughtful reason for doing so. Nothing is more hurtful than if the accusation for using the expression is incorrect and only based on assumptions and rumours.

If someone says, "It's nothing to be proud of" to you, think carefully before you answer.

Maybe the right thing to do is to test yourself every now and then. How would I react if someone told me that, "It's nothing to be proud of"?

If someone address you with the expression, "I'm proud of you", and you know it's well meant, then you feel the warmth.

Being honest, which, of course, you are, never use the expression "I am proud of you" for anyone, unless you mean it full heartedly.

We know it is warming when someone uses that expression with us, and we know it is well meant and deserved.

However, if you feel that it's not honestly meant, or maybe it's somewhat sarcastic, it can sear quite strongly.

Maybe you should tidy up your own use of these types of compliments.

How often do you yourself use the expression, "I'm proud of you"?

Think about how you would react if you were to hear these five words from someone who means a lot to you; wouldn't it warm you?

Pride shines out of the eyes; the purpose is achieved.

The goal is achieved. The bigger the offer has been and the more you have sacrificed to reach the goal, the prouder you are.

I think we have all been acquainted with the good feeling of pride.

This type of pride is just as big whatever the case. It's not a matter of the size of the feat. Everything is personal and proportional.

Whether the first time you balanced on a bike, the distinction you got in sport or other milestones, the pride is personal and proportional to the efforts you made to reach the goal.

The most important type of pride is the one on behalf of others. It gives double pleasure, especially if you have personally been part of that which the person in question deserves the expression for. "You can be proud of that".

We all have a hint of personal pride, and that's both right and important.

When this type of pride gets overdeveloped, however, it becomes difficult to deal with.

With an overdeveloped personality it feels good to express that one is proud of what one has done.

It's often the way the pride is expressed which matters. "Modesty is a virtue" is an expression.

Do you act with a superior attitude because you are afraid of making a fool of yourself, or of exposing yourself? Has it something to do with taking yourself too seriously?

Personal pride should not be overdeveloped.

In my opinion, the most sympathetic pride is the one shown on behalf of others – but it must be honest.

****

MY FOOD FOR THOUGHT ON PRIDE

PRIDE

The Pride you have on behalf of others is the best form of Pride.

2014

PRIDE AND ARROGANCE

If people looked more closely at how the encyclopaedia describes Pride and Arrogance and left these burdensome traits behind, many would be perceived as far more sympathetic.

February 2019

PRIDE I

Your personal Pride should not be overdeveloped.

2020

PRIDE II

Little can hurt more than if someone tells you:
"That's nothing to be proud of".

2023

UNDERSTANDING

October 2013

Think what a difference it would make if we humans one day really understood one another. This is, of course, not black and white, as we mostly understand one another – at least with regard to major issues; but differences and disputes often occur because of our thinking that we have understood everything without this being the case; especially when it has to do with details, and small but important nuances.

There is usually no harm intended by either party, but often nuances causing misleading results.

Does this mean that in general we don't understand each other, and that there would be a marked difference in results on the day when we really do manage to understand one another? Yes, I believe so. We often don't understand one another, and this leads to unforeseen challenges in our narrow everyday lives, as well as in a larger national, international, and global context.

First, we must recognise what is meant by fully understanding one another.

Here it isn't just that we speak different languages. Misunderstandings can be fertile ground for disagreements, even when both parties communicating, seemingly speak the same language.

In simple communication the main issues are usually understood. Nuances and details, however, often count for more than you can imagine.

This is what we must realize if any of the content in this reflection is to make sense.

You must realize that when you delve into a communication, nuances can easily be downplayed or disappear, and the deeper meaning often is not evident or understood.

Many of us can't see this, which is probably only to the good, as we don't all have to delve so deeply into details.

I have my own experience when it comes to different languages and understanding.

My wife is Swiss, and since she comes from Geneva her mother tongue is French.

I don't speak French and have for various reasons never had the inclination to learn this language, so our communication takes place in English. In both our cases, this was not the language used at the beginning of our lives; it was not our own and we both had to learn it.

She has lived in Spain for more than forty years and was married to an Englishman for more than twenty, whereas my English comes from school in Norway, living abroad in a predominantly English environment and from business.

Her vocabulary is extensive, whereas mine is more limited. Despite this, I find that our everyday communication functions very well.

We have also been part of the "vintage" category for some time now, and this undoubtedly has its advantages as regards communication, since maturity often means acquiring more tolerance, at least according to yourself.

It becomes easier to make allowances for misunderstandings, when communicating in a language which is foreign to both parties, and when you have a smidgen of tolerance.

Understanding is not always positive, however.

The so-called know-it-all, who supposedly understand it all, aren't necessarily entirely likeable, but this doesn't mean, of course, that those who have no understanding whatsoever, automatically can be labelled as likeable.

Expressions like, "I understand your point of view", or such, are frequently used in diplomatic circles, where it often has to do with making approaches through give and take. When results are to be achieved through understanding and tact, details and nuances are important.

In political contexts, appeals are often made to show understanding, thus calling for diplomatic solutions.

Can we learn to understand one another better?

For me it's quite clear that we can, if we first acknowledge that it is often understanding the details and nuances, which make for a better relationship.

If you are conscious of this, you can in various contexts, through the seeking of common understanding, go a long way towards reaching more agreement.

MY FOOD FOR THOUGHT ON UNDERSTANDING I

UNDERSTANDING I

Those who think that I don't have it, have evidently not Understood - that things have been let happen which I later saw should have been halted. For the very simple reason that development takes place through sacrifice and vision, not by putting a calculated stop to the mission. It has cost to sow - the profits maybe low - but it's worth the Understanding I have gathered up to now.

UNDERSTANDING II

A well-known expression is that the most dangerous are those who themselves do not Understand that they do not Understand. However it does not mean that you are blameless even if you admit that you don't Understand.

Nov. 2019

UNDERSTANDING III

For those who do not Understand, no problems exist.

July 2019

UNDERSTANDING AND DECISIONS

All Decisions, if they are meant to have any value, must be based on Understanding, thus on the will to Understand the matter and the parties involved.

March 2013

PRESTIGE

April 2013

Here it is a matter of your own reputation and then it becomes both personal and difficult. It is unfortunately so that what becomes personal can easily develop into becoming uncomfortable. It is a protected world, where others have no right to be; or have they?

For some, prestige has no meaning in their daily lives, whereas for others it is vital and counts every hour of the day, all year round.

It is this prestige I'd like to dwell on a bit. I've experienced various sides of it, but I must admit that my experiences haven't always been positive. Not that they have been important to me, but I have found people concerned with prestige to be navigating in their own world. If they themselves are aware of this it must be their own decision, but perhaps prestige acts as a protective shell, something you can hide behind in order not to be too transparent? Perhaps its prestige which makes them function and gives them purpose in their everyday life?

The most important aspect is not what they themselves represent, but what they believe they represent to those around them. The strange thing is that if they don't come across as people who share their values, then they pull out their entire arsenal, as it becomes important for them to leave a prestige-filled impression. Is it done to impress or, once again, is it to hide something?

There is often no limit to what others offer by way of

conversation, and certain pet topics are frequently repeated. I've thought about whether there is something deeper behind this.

Is it the case that people who seem to have experienced most things in life, feel that it's still important to give the impression that they have done even more than they really have? Is it a built-in inadequacy or perhaps an additional need to hide something, which must be satisfied?

Up until now, it has all been about verbal prestige, but that's only one of its facets. Expressions like, "that lends prestige to the person in question" or, "that's a prestigious position" speak for themselves and carry no judgements.

Used in such contexts, there are no negative thoughts behind them.

What about the type of prestige, which has to do with trends and status?

Trends are normally something which concerns the younger generation, and though they are seldom so far along in life that prestige - the way I see it - has taken root in their consciousness.

Young people just want whatever it is because others have it, and because it's trendy. This is rightly called peer pressure.

I've got a bit of a problem seeing the difference between prestige and status, but I am sure there is a difference. The struggle for social status, for instance, has more to do with living up to other people's standards, and the wish not to be different.

Status symbol is the name given to that which you acquire outwardly, in the form of prestigious cars, boats, etc. This type of prestige goes deep with a lot of people.

I remember well, when my then common-law wife, who a year later became my lawfully wedded wife, got her first Hyundai Coupé in 1997. She bought it on my recommendation. I had been around to Oslo's car dealerships with my son-in-law, to have a look at their selection. I don't remember the name of the dealership, but we noticed a car I thought looked very stylish in the car park outside. It turned out to be a Hyundai Coupé which belonged to the sales manager and was the only one at the time of its kind to have been imported. I talked to my wife on the phone that same afternoon and she started her local enquiries immediately.

By chance she heard that a car dealership in the town, Cuevas del Almanzora, half an hour's drive from where we lived, had become a Hyundai agent. She ordered the car unseen and had it delivered after a fortnight.

My surprise was great when she met me at the airport with her newly acquired car after my visit to Norway. She hadn't mentioned anything to me about the purchase.

My wife has since had two further cars of the Coupé type and changed just a few months ago to a smaller model, the i30. I have had two Hyundai Santa Fe's. The last one I had for seven years, and we can't express how happy we are and have been with all of them. I'm not being paid by Hyundai for these superlatives, even though it might seem so.

I won't mention what brand of car I'm currently driving, as it might upset my idea of prestige.

So where does prestige enter it?

Well, it took several years before you could talk openly about the Hyundai brand in Norway. You also didn't see many of them on the roads and there definitely wasn't any prestige or status involved in driving this brand. In fact, for some it was rather embarrassing. Prestige and status meant driving Audi, Mercedes and BMW; only then did you belong.

Eventually more Santa Fes were being used as taxis, and today we probably talk about both KIA and Hyundai as drivable vehicles; but there's no prestige in driving either of them, as I understand – at least not in Norway.

No, the similarity or difference between prestige and status, I can't seem to come to grips with, so I'll try to stick with pure prestige.

I can't help mentioning an example, which must have gone quite deep. A friend of mine, an employer, once told me of a work problem.

In a difficult economic period lay-offs became necessary. A particular person holding a high position, had for years performed impeccably for the firm, but finally the day of his redundancy had arrived. The person in question – who understood the reason behind the lay-offs –, offered to take a drastic drop in salary or to change his position internally, but insisted his title must be kept.

I'm inclined to draw the conclusion that it must have been his social status, as well as prestige, which caused this reaction.

Here we go again, prestige and status.

Something more down to earth: in 2002 the biggest oil spill in the history of Spain, Portugal and France took place. Hundreds if not thousands of kilometres of beaches were destroyed, when an enormous tanker broke in half and went down on the Spanish north-west coast. The name of the tanker was "Prestige" and it spilled 63,000 tons of oil.

In my thinking, prestige doesn't guarantee anything at all.

****

MY FOOD FOR THOUGHT ON PRESTIGE

PRESTIGE

Prestige gives no guarantee whatsoever. The tanker "Prestige" went down in 2002 and 63.000 tons of oil leaked out.

2013

PRESTIGIOUS AND TOUCHY

A Prestigious person can often appear Touchy.

January 2019

POMPOUS I

Do some people appear Pompous to cover an inferiority complex?

May 2019

POMPOUS II

Feel pity with those who believe that respect increases with their Pompous behaviour. I believe most people's opinion is the opposite.

Nov. 2019

TOLERANCE

2017

First, to be very plain about the word tolerance: it means to withstand and hold out, not physical strength. "Tolerance is the ability to withstand living with those who have different opinions and attitudes and who then acts; in other words, those which you do not usually accept".

This should be a reflection for all of us.

Most of us will add something more direct to being tolerant, something more to the point. Either you tolerate this or that, or you don't.

Seen from that angle we clearly speak of something black or white or what?

That is not the case.

The description of tolerance states that we are talking about a balancing act.

You tolerate to a greater or lesser extent, which I consider is good.

In other words, I claim for a fact that tolerance is not black or white.

Tolerance is a balancing act and Compromise is the weight on the scale making it balance.

Compromise must be part of the balancing act.

It is impossible to perform a balancing act without adding the ingredient of give and take, in other words, Compromise, and that I think is good.

Imagine how well those who mean they are tolerant feel. Such an attitude becomes subjective, as others undoubtedly may have a divergent view.

Standing a little further away, a little more on the outside, pretending to have a more objective view, may give you an easier opportunity to make a statement about the person's ability to act with tolerance.

How we as individuals relate to tolerance is of the greatest importance for our identity.

As I have made Compromise part of the heading and claim it as a condition for tolerance to be practised, I will dwell a little on this word.

One explanation goes as follows: "A Compromise is a result of actions where no one of the parties gets its will 100%, but everyone gets something".

Apart from Love, Compromise, may be one of the most important words.

Even when using the expression "unconditional love", there is a need for a little Compromise at time.

Reaching out your hand to your enemy is, I believe, not the same as turning the other cheek. In principle I am totally for the one with the cheek, but life experience has taught me that this approach seldom results in success. The reason being that man is his own worst enemy.

On the other hand, to reach out a hand as a start, particularly when it is done with good will, does not result in an either/or situation, meaning that you either get a slap when you turn the other cheek, or you do not.

Maybe I have reached this conclusion after having had dogs most of my life, before I became a pensioner.

From when I was only six, my best friend was our English Setter.

Having to do with dogs, you know that the best way to approach a strange dog, is to carefully stretch out your hand. You will quickly experience if this invitation to closer contact is successful.

Luckily, I have still both hands with full sets of fingers and have only the best experience with this approach.

I will not dwell further with this comparison. Everyone has their own experience, but what I try to emphasize is that the situation is not black or white.

Unfortunately, we humans have a sad tendency to make things black or white. Everything becomes easier by making things black or white, but also thus more incorrect.

A Balanced Tolerance with the aid of Compromise is necessary. Give a little and take a little, none of the parties feel they are with their back against the wall.

To simplify everything is not always the best solution, understood as looking at the situation as black or white. Because of such simplifications, often unnecessary discontent occurs, resulting in Tolerance with the aid of Compromise being put to a big test.

Tolerance is an ingredient in a variety of situations, without me dwelling to much on it. The total lack of tolerance related to the acceptance of different religions, is probably what has caused the biggest challenges on our planet throughout time.

Maybe not so strange as this is where we find the most

fanatics, clearly examples of people with black or white opinions.

****

MY FOOD FOR THOUGHT ON TOLERANCE

TOLERANCE I

Tolerance stands for patience and the acceptance of other people's opinions.
Where the ceiling is high, the volume is always greater and there's more room to play with. Opposites attract it is said,
and there's probably a lot of truth in that, but not without tolerance.

From a wedding speech in 2005

TOLERANCE III

It costs, but you don't lose much of yourself by being Tolerant.

2018

TOLERANCE AND BALANCE

If you are Tolerant without being taken for granted, you can achieve a better Balance in yourself.

April 2019

TOLERANCE AND COMPROMISE I

Tolerance is a balancing act and Compromise is the weight on the scales that makes it balance.

2016

LOVE

2015

This heading has remained empty for a long time, a very long time. Not because I couldn't get started on it, but – and this is most likely my explanation in a nutshell – because love is probably the world's most significant word, a word we ought to have the greatest respect for.

You can't get started on a reflection about love just like that.

Practically all types of literature are concerned, at least partly, with love.

Normally not only with the simple emotional attraction between individual people, but often with the one lightly seasoned with the sensual. The sometimes almost animal attraction can create a suspense which makes the reader concentrate. I'll put this part – which is of course important, but which is far from being all that love has to offer – behind me first.

I'll never forget my first contact with the literary insight into the matter.

In the bookcase on the far wall of the sitting room in the "old" house at Landøya where I grew up, about a metre away from the keyboard of the grand piano, was the book: "Lady Chatterley's Lover".

At the time the book was published in Norwegian in 1952 when I was about thirteen, I couldn't really relate to the word love, of course. Even though I have no memory of it, I must somehow have understood the word, but I can't remember growing up with any special warmth from being spoiled with love. Nor was the opposite in any way the case; but I probably saw myself as someone who had fallen between two stools in one form or other.

Nothing wrong with having a stepfather as such, but perhaps there wasn't quite enough room for all three of us at the beginning during those post-war days.

Anyway, as with millions of other readers, the book became my first literary contact with sexual matters, and we'll leave it at that.

The sexual part of love I learnt to understand early on, while the part related to its combination with deeper feelings took somewhat longer.

It must have been a copy of the first edition of the book in Norwegian that they had in their bookcase. As far as I remember, it was illustrated with drawings, albeit without any erotic angle, as I recall.

As it was, at times, being carefully coaxed out of the bookcase for a closer acquaintance, it was always put back with the greatest of care, so that its having been "borrowed" wouldn't be discovered.

At approximately the same time, I seem to recall that the pornographic magazine "Cocktail" caused great excitement, when on rare occasions you came across a copy.

It might, of course, be tempting to continue along this track, but where should I then draw the line. It could well be that, in that case, I would get carried away, which would undoubtedly lead me astray, as there is more to love than the erotic.

As mentioned above, it took somewhat longer to gain an understanding of its combination with the deeper feelings of love, and there is really no reason why I should know something which others don't know about the word love, which in my opinion is the most important one in our vocabulary.

It is just great to look up its various definitions, and there are lots of them when it comes to love. The love of whom, of what and its various forms, is described in detail, which, of course, isn't strange when you think of the significance of love. In practically all forms of literature, love is present, and where it appears it is given special attention.

Without being able to put my finger on it, I believe it's just as important to be able to give as to be able to receive love; and here, as in so many other situations in life, it's a question of balance.

I'm probably skating on thin ice here. In this case as far as love goes, to give and receive won't seem as right and true, if there's talk about conscious control, in other words if it's all about determination and not feeling, will it?

No wonder the topic is a complicated one.

Love between two people is, in my opinion, unreservedly dependent on honesty, tolerance, and respect for one an- other, if the relationship is to function.

I have long been convinced of this, and so I quote in reversed order, an excerpt from a speech I made to my nephew, Thomas, and his, Trine, on their wedding day, on the 6th of August, 2005.

Respect for one another:
A well-known and important expression, which is far-reaching as well as being an extremely important ingredient in dealing with the many challenges of married life. The good thing is that you don't need any experience to respect one another. Here all you need is awareness. Remind yourself from time to time what having respect for one another means in its broadest sense and acting accordingly.

Tolerance:
This word stands for patience and the acceptance of other people's opinions. Where the ceiling is high, the volume is always greater and there's more room to play. Opposites attract it is said, and there's probably a lot of truth in that, but not without tolerance.

Honesty:
Honesty is also not to be frowned upon. Suspicion and jealousy are poison and can be hidden dangers on the road of life. If you make honesty part of your daily agenda, as well as having a good part of tolerance and respect for one another, many of life's sharp edges can be blunted.

Love, last but not least:
Saying I love you is allowed; and it is not forbidden to say it several times a day. Can that really be necessary, some of you may ask, we are married after all, so it must go without saying. The fact is, it doesn't go without saying. We need

all the encouragement we can get from these three words, and it always does you good to hear them, preferably several times a day.

For me, the touch of love is important. To hold a hand, to touch and feel contact.

Perhaps the best expression about love between people is the one that says: “It falls as easily on a turd as on a lily”.

Love is the food of life.

****

MY FOOD FOR THOUGHT ON LOVE

LOVE I

Perhaps the best thing about Love between people is the phrase:
"It falls as easily on a turd as on a lily."
Love is the best food of life.

2014

LOVE II

Love based on false feelings has nothing to do with real Love.

April 2014

LOVE, LAST BUT NOT LEAST

Saying I love you is allowed, and it is not forbidden to say it several times a day. Can that really be necessary, some of us may ask, we are married after all, so it must go without saying.
The fact is it doesn't go without saying.
We need all the encouragement we can get from these tree words.
and it always feels good to hear them, preferably several times a day.

From a wedding speech in 2005

LOVE AND COMPROMISE

Even with expressions like unconditional Love, there is sometimes.
a need for Compromise.

2016

WILL

May 2014

Unlike physical strength, I see the human will as an unbelievably strong resource. A strong-willed person often gets that term just because she or he stands for having a strong will.

First, we must clear away the will related to stubbornness, the one occurring specially in kids and adolescents.

Not that this type of will necessarily disappears because of you have grown up; but for those that it applies to there will always be problems.

The will I have in mind is the positive will, the one that makes thoughts and meanings grow to new heights.

The will to understand is one of several good examples of a positive will. You may as well call it the ground-breaking will.

If you are to reach a goal you have set for yourself, whatever the type, the will must be there.

It's not the case at all that if only the will is there, you automatically reach all the goals you have set for yourself.

A will is only one of the ingredients needed to do so, but maybe the one that at the end of the day is the condition needed to put your thoughts and meanings forward.

Back to the positive will, the will to understand.

For me it's totally clear that no challenges can be overcome if you don't have the will to do so, and if you want to be able to overcome them, you must understand both the challenges and those involved.

Your will is a power which, when properly used, is incredibly strong.

People glowing with positive willpower normally have their understanding in order.

But and this is important, it must be a positive, natural will and not one which is forced.

The will can, in some people, be destructive and effacing if seen in conjunction with negativity – negative will.

In this context it is a matter of people with weak willpower, or people with no will. No positivity can come from having weak willpower or being without a will.

I have little experience of how these expressions are used in daily life, but I presume that they are quite similar when it comes to performance, although they are of different gravity.

If you have week willpower, the will still plays a role, although minor. If, on the contrary, you are without will, it means that you are devoid of will. In this case you are badly off for action.

Anyhow, all this is just a lot of theory, of course. How the will is perceived by each one of us in our daily life, remains something we should not dwell on too often.

There are plenty of other things our brain must cope with.

MY FOOD FOR THOUGHT ON WILL

THE WILL TO UNDERSTAND

The Will to Understand as well as the desire and faith that you shall succeed, is a condition for reaching your goals.

THE WILL TO WIN

It is easy to remind yourself that the W in the Will is the first letter, in the same way that Winning starts with a W. That is exactly what it is all about. If you lack the Will to Win, it is like giving up. In this context it's about overcoming the challenges.

January 2019

WILL AND UNWILLINGNESS

The positive Will and the Will to understand are the most important Wills - while Unwillingness will always be negative.

WILL IS FUNDAMENTAL

The Will to understand is Fundamental. If the Will is failing because the understanding fails, the result is halting.

May 2014

FSC
www.fsc.org
MIX
Papir fra
ansvarlige kilder
Paper from
responsible sources
FSC® C105338